TAILS OF A
WOODSWOMAN II

PATRICIA ANDERSON

Order this book online at www.trafford.com
or email orders@trafford.com

Most Trafford titles are also available at major online book retailers.

Print information available on the last page.

ISBN: 978-1-4907-2265-8 (sc)
ISBN: 978-1-4907-2267-2 (hc)
ISBN: 978-1-4907-2266-5 (e)

Library of Congress Control Number: 2013923683

Trafford rev. 09/17/2015

 www.trafford.com

North America & international
toll-free: 1 888 232 4444 (USA & Canada)
fax: 812 355 4082

Front Cover illustration

Done by

Cathy Tatom

@ Crazie Creek

(325)-236-2373

Cjctatom@yahoo.com

TABLE OF CONTENTS

TAILS TOLD BY OTHERS

TAILS OF THE SPIRIT

TAIL PIPES

The Conclusion

DEDICATION

These writings are dedicated to my Grandma Myrtle Bathurst. As a young child I would sit wide eyed as Grandma would tell her true stories of being raised in southern Florida. Her stories ranged from having to pull adult chickens from the mouth of large snakes and how one night a Florida panther stalked her. She had been raised in Florida over 100 years ago.

It is my wish that her story telling abilities I have captured in my own true stories of Florida.

Dating Tails

F INALLY OUR PATHS CROSSED AGAIN it had been 5 long years. In that time frame Sue had moved and I had traveled west more than once. We were very pleased to find each other again. We had both returned back to Astor, Florida where we had originally met. We chatted for hours. Then came the conversation of men. "Who was I dating now?" I laughed loudly and began to share some dating stories with Sue. I first told her about the cute guy on the Flagler fishing pier. He had arrived to the pier shortly after I had and began fishing nearby. He attempted small talk with me and I might add that he had stirred my interest. Then the fish started to bite. I caught one (a bluefish) then he caught one. Then it happened; Sue stated "What happened?" He took his dentures out and chunked them into the bottom of his tackle box. In an attempt to clarify, Sue said "Did he have a container for them?" I finished the story with the fact that he had tossed them into his tackle box next to a few dried worms and miscellaneous tackle (clearly he fresh water fished with the same box). We continued to fish, at which point he looked at me and explained that his dentures were costly and he didn't want to lose them to the sea. Thirty minutes later, (as I now attempted to ignore him) a pizza arrived he had ordered delivered to the pier. Well some woman might have found that romantic, I was slightly impressed until he reached into his dirty tackle box to retrieve his full set of dentures, placing then back in his mouth to chew his pizza. I was grossed out! He kindly offered me some of his pizza; I refused and stood frozen trying not to look in his direction. Once full, he followed his established routine and back into the tackle box-the dentures went. This time he added the statement "I know I look a little young to have dentures, but I had ta get em, cause I had real bad case of pyorrhea". It was that statement that ended my fishing trip, he attempted to get my phone number, I ignored his request and half trotted off the pier.

Then there was the guy I met on Christmas Day, in the local restaurant. in Colorado Springs. We had motorcycles riding and dog ownership in common. We shared a lot of stories. And before I left we exchanged phone numbers. Later that week he called and invited me to movies and snacks. I agreed and he asked me to come to his house because he was doing laundry. (I fantasized about going to the theater and dinner at the local diner). When I arrived at his house I notice he had his pajama bottoms on. I assumed he was waiting for his blue jeans to dry.

That wasn't the case. Instead he had rented movies, handed me a bowl of popcorn. Then he began wandering back in forth to the laundry room, I never did meet his dogs and he never did change into his jeans. As the movie finished he entered the room and asked if I was going to spend the night? I abruptly left laughing about how dating had changed.

Then there was the guy up in West Virginia who had bought my 1st book from a friend, took one look at my picture on the back cover (of me holding a bass I had caught), and now he was hooked. He called me at least daily (sometimes 5 times a day) for 5 months. Finally, I had business in a nearby state, so I agreed to come to West Virginia to meet him. He picked me up at my Motel room, took me to Dinner then to meet his friends. All was going well until we arrived at his home. I noticed he parked his truck close to the brushes, as if to hide his vehicle. Then he said to me "Run into the house"! I took a quick survey of his yard to see what I was suppose to out run. I saw the big rock cliff with a creek flowing in front of it. It appeared to be a tranquil setting. In Florida, if we tell someone to run, it is because a gator, snake or bear may be present. My eyes scanned the yard again. I came up with nothing.

So I asked him the obvious question "What am I running from?" He stated my ex girlfriend. There were no other houses nearby and no other people, but I was compliant with his request and ran to his trailer. I felt a bit uncomfortable in his house as I wondered about this old girlfriend. I wondered what she looked like and if I was in any danger. I made it approximately 30 minutes, and then I requested to return to my motel room. The exit from his house was as strange as the entrance; his little terrier dog has issues with people when they attempt to exit his home. He had to hold the dog as I ran to the truck in order not to be bitten on the ankle by his little terror terrier dog or attacked by the old girlfriend (where ever she might be hiding). By the end of that adventure, I was truly ready to RUN my ass back to Florida as quickly as possible.

Sue and I laughed and cut up about the stories I had just told, then she shared a story about when she and Glenn first starting dating. Glenn was my old neighbor so I knew about his strange fetish for rattlesnakes. He must have been a snake in a past life. Glenn would go out of his way to avoid killing a diamond back rattlesnake. He would become deeply upset when he saw a dead rattlesnake on the side of the road. He truly connected with diamondback rattlesnakes. When he spotted a rattlesnake he would take a small stick and knock the snake out, then carry it around to show this knocked out snake to others. Sue explained that on one of their first dates, they were riding around the Ocala National Forest when a rattlesnake appeared in the road. Sue added, "it was a big one"! Glenn leaped from Sue's car and knocked the snake out then proceeded to approach the car with this approx 4-foot or bigger, temporally unconscious snake. Sue freaked! He insisted on taking this poisonous slightly dazed snake home. Finally came the compromise—Sue drove, while Glenn held the snake outside the passenger side window. The snake was placed in an aquarium at Glenn's home. Two days later when Glenn came home from work, oddly the snake lay dead.

Sue and Glenn are still together (after 15 years). Glenn continues to knock out rattlesnakes and bring them home. As for Sue, she has become an expert at killing rattlesnakes. Go figure?

THE SMILING MILE

IT WAS MARCH AND MY friends from Michigan; Paul and Vicky had arrived for their yearly trip to Florida. This year they were accompanied by another couple from Michigan. It was great that we were all together again. We sat up to the wee hours of the morning exchanging stories about the past and the present. The next morning we all slept in, except Paul. He awakened to a crisp Florida winter day and decided to take a walk with Heidi dog down the mile dirt road. So Heidi dog and Paul walked down the road waving at the neighbors as they drove past him. Then something caught his eye; he looked down to the left side of his sweatshirt, in disbelief. Right there clinging to his hooded sweatshirt was some teeth, stuck and hanging. He laughed aloud! It seems he left the house grabbing the sweatshirt that lay by the bed not realizing that his wife Vicky had evidently laid her upper dentures on his sweatshirt—they stuck. Now being married for over 30 years, he realized that if he can't get his wife to walk with him, he'll just take her teeth. And he did! We all wondered what the neighbors thought as they drove by Paul happily walking with Heidi dog with a set of dentures stuck to his sweatshirt.

THE CLUMSY NEIGHBOR

MY BOYFRIEND AND I HAD lived only a few months at my new home in the Ocala National forest, when we met a new neighbor-Glenn. Glenn worked and resided at the youth camp located across the lake from my farm. One particular evening, Glenn arrived at my house soaking wet holding a beer can in his left hand, stating "I just saved my own life"! He explained that while driving his John boat to my farm he spotted large gator swimming in the lake and made a quick turn around to go back and see the gator. Apparently, this turn was too quick for him and he fell out of his own boat, holding his beer can still upright while his boat circled around him. After several attempts to cut off the boat that was still turning in circles around him he was able to grap the side of the boat and climb back in-saving his own life and not spilling a drop of his beer. Glenn made it known he was proud of both rescues (the beer and himself). After he calmed down and dried off, he went back home. I must confuse I was beginning to wonder about our new neighbor.

The next day Glenn returned via the same boat. This time he was dry, so he had managed to stay in the boat for his entire trip to the farm. However, he was carrying what appeared to be a large glass pickle jar (by the lid) in one hand and his beer in the other. As Glenn began to run closer up the hill, I noticed what was in this glass pickle jar— my clumsy neighbor was carrying. It was a diamondback rattlesnake!

Somehow, Gregg had managed to squash this large live, pissed off rattlesnake into a glass jar and running up the hill to show us.

My boyfriend, who is very scared of snakes especially the poisonous ones, met him in the yard and insisted he and his pickle jar return home. Glenn, feelings hurt did indeed climb back into his boat and return home. I quickly realized that living near Glenn may become a bit challenging. The old woods expression seem to apply here "YOU GOTTA BE TOUGH IF YOU'RE GONNA BE STUPID!"

THE MELT DOWN

A S WE APPROACHED THE SWIM lake located in Astor Park, Florida (the locals frequently refer to this lake as skinny dip pond. I explained to my date Lee Roy that located across the highway was Billy's Bay, the part of the Ocala Forest well known for it's black bear population.

It is important to note that Lee Roy was a well-portioned physical fit guy with a multitude of tattoos to accent his muscles. I noticed that in public places, he was immediately noticed by all, and most men respected him. He had that air of tough guy energy around him.

The lake was located behind a tree line just off the highway. You had to pull off the side of the road and hike down to it. As we hiked down to the lake and I babbled on about the bear population, Lee Roy pointed over to the side of the lake and stated "isn't that a bear over there". Sure enough it was, a large black bear batting the water at the fish. My response was "Cool" we can sit and watch him. Lee Roy began to perspire a lot on his face and forehead and suggested we go now! I attempted to calm him by explaining that the Florida black bear is very nearsighted and he can't see us. In addition, I added that there was no wind, therefore this bear couldn't smell us either. Lee Roy began to pitch a fit, insisting we leave now. His face was turning red and sweat was dripping everywhere. He clearly was having a meltdown! In a final attempt to calm him, I explained that I had an injured knee and all he had to do was run faster than me. He didn't find that comment funny either. So I reluctantly went back to the truck. That is when Lee Roy started to confess. He said that 20 years ago he had entered a "tough man" contest in Ohio. Stated he had scrapped together all the cash he had to enter this contest. A win would pay off $1000.00. He stated that the rule was that he had to enter a cage with a black bear and stay for 60 seconds. He thought at the time it would be easy money. He proceeded to tell me that immediately after entering the cage the bear knocked him down and began banging his shoulders on the floor of the cage. Stated this bear broke his ribs, his nose and basically beat his ass. He had to be dragged by his feet out of the cage and taken to the hospital for a few days. Although I could greatly appreciate his fears, holding the laughter inside was virtually impossible. At first I stated "no way" no one in his right mind would get into a cage with a wild animal, right? He continued to tell his story and then stated "I thought I had got over this fear, clearly I havent". Laughter ripped out of me as I attempted to ask him why he ever thought he was tougher than a wild animal, but I struggled to get the question out of my mouth before I went into belly roaring laughter! Just then it hit me I have been sleeping with this fool, oh no, the phrase "Welcome to my world" danced in my head.

He kept telling me his story really wasn't funny, so I made every attempt to look out the window of the truck and not laugh. That didn't work either! As his melt down faded away, I could see he was becoming angry at my laughter. So I suggested we go to another lake several miles down the road.

We arrived at the other lake, I got out and attempted to lure him down to the lake. It was a great spring Florida day and wildlife was abundant. There were deer, raccoon and a little gator at the lakeside. After he finished a few beers, he did start to leave the side of the truck and join me at the lake. It appeared his meltdown had subsided, all was calm for now.

As we began to leave, we drove only ½ mile down the road when another bear appeared on the side of the road. That did it for me, laugher roared from my lips, suddenly the truck spun sideways as he hit the gas pedal in extreme fear and we flew sideways several miles to the pavement. I tried to explain, but he just would not listen, that this was the first time ever, that I have seen two different bears in the same day. I added the universe clearly has a sense of humor when it comes to "Whose the tough guy now?"

THE HAIRY CATCH

SATURDAY WAS HERE AT LAST; my boyfriend and I had taken 1-week vacation to just go fishing. We had decided we would pick 7 Florida Lakes and fish a different one each day. Today was the beginning of our adventure. We loaded up my 14-foot homemade johnboat, appropriately named "The SS Leak" and headed to the Lake.

Once on the lake, my boyfriend mentioned that he had this secret weapon borrowed (just last night) from his fishing buddy. He then pulled an 8-inch lure from his tackle box. He explains that this lure only costs $15.00 and had a built in rattle. As I examined this mammoth lure closer, I noticed that it had not one, not two, not three but 4 that's right 4 three prong hooks. I immediately thought to myself, you know you're a southern if your favorite fishing lure has more hooks then you have teeth. I decided not to speak that aloud, for fear he wouldn't find it funny. I teased him about the lure and that it resembled a device used to scrap the bottom of the lake, and then I spoke the challenge "I still can catch more fish than you and that fancy $15.00 lure". The challenge was on!

I sat at the front of the boat, casting my rubber worm ahead of the boat. Occasionally, I would stop to bail the boat. You see, the SS Leak had clearly seen better days, and now the ribbed bottom leaked.

I secretly enjoyed being able to soak my feet and fish too. But this fishing/ foot soaking wasn't for everyone.

Then came that rattle sound right near my right ear. At first, I didn't realize what it was, that is until the second cast. It was that fancy, over hooked $ 15.00 lure flying extremely close to my scalp. After his third cast, I turned and informed my boyfriend, just how pissed I would be if that tangled in my hair. By the look on his face he didn't appreciate the scolding. All I could think of, was how much scalp and hair that fancy lure could rip out of my head. I didn't care to endure that experience at all.

I turned back around and proceeded to cast my rubber worm, now more than ever desperately wanting to catch more fish then the expansive lure would attract. After a few casts, I noticed that I didn't hear my boyfriend fishing anymore. I thought to myself, oh great I must have really pissed him off insulting his casting abilities. I waiting a few moments, finally curiosity got the best of me and I turned and looked behind me. There he was in all his glory, using one hand to hold the lure (so I wouldn't hear the rattle) and using the other hand to try to dig it out of his own hair.

It seems his last cast had put that fancy $15.00 lure in direct contact with his scalp—not mine. Tears ran down my cheeks as I tried to stop the laughter.

I knew he wasn't seriously hurt. Just his fishing pride was on the line right now, literally. Suddenly I just couldn't maintain any longer. In a laughing voice I said "What cha doing honey?" he repeated "I'll get it". "Okay". I turned and attempted to fish, my belly shook as I tried to hold my belly laughter, and it was just too funny. After 15 minutes, I was able to control laughter enough to turn and assist him in removing the lure from his hair. I had to cut all the hair around the hooks to get it to release. Apparently, after I had insisted he not cast towards me, he had thrown this lure with a little extra thrust, only to catch his own head in the passing. When we finally, removed the now hairy lure, my boyfriend cut it off his line and placed hair and all, into the bottom of the tackle box. You know, I never, saw that lure again.

Imagine that!

THE ATTACK

IT WAS A DAY FOR an adventure, so Paul, Vicky and I set out by
boat to explore all 12 of the lakes that adjoin Lake Sellers. We
borrowed the neighbor's boat since the SS Leak that I owned had
a tendency to take in water. For short adventures it was okay but for
all day it would surely sink. Off we went in a aluminum 14 foot boat
with a 25 horse motor on it. Paul and I took turns driving and Vicky
just enjoyed the sun on her back and the wind through her hair. The
last lake had a pretty sand beach and crystal clear water, (in Florida
that is usually a sign of spring fed lake). It was. We swam and explored
the beach since it told of recent parties, by evidence of empty beer cans
and fire pits. All was well until the trip back. In the middle of one of
the lakes, we discovered it was very shallow and muddy, we had to lift
the motor because it started to drag in the mud. I requested for Paul
to get out of the boat in this muddy lake and pull us a short distance
to a deeper spot. Paul reluctantly agreed, as he attempted to step out
of the boat, we heard a bang to the side of the boat, then another.
Paul looked over the boat and said, "We're under attack!". That got
my attention! I confess I felt some relief when I realized that it was
a strange looking fish, not a gator. Paul quickly sat down away from
the side of the boat and peeked over the boat edge at the same time
I did. The boat dipped down and scared us all. Suddenly, another
bang to the boat then another. At this point I noticed Vicky sitting

in the middle of the boat with her arms scretched out to each side of the boat. Vicky's hands clutched at the boat sides and the top of her hands were white. She was desperately trying to keep the boat from being taken from her from this monster sea creature. I would be lying if I said I wasn't scared. I was! I attempted to reassure everyone that this had never happened before. Although truthful, it didn't seem to have the calming effect needed at the time. I witnessed another hit to the boat and realized it was a dark colored fish. We had wondered off our original path and were now in swallow waters where the mudfish bed. These slimly black 2 foot fish (that resemble catfish), were clearly pissed we had unwittingly violated their beds and they were attempting to run us off. We all agreed they didn't have to keep hitting the boat, we were already ready to leave. And leave we did. Paul and I dug in the mud with paddles to propel the boat forward and after 20 minutes we were afloat again. We all remained silent as we went across Lake Sellers to the house; Vicky still clutching the boat edges with white fist. Finally, we made it to dry land—relief and safe. That evening, I told this adventure to some local boys, they stared in disbelief, making the comments that they would like to try the drugs we were on. No one believed that we had somehow gone off course, and adventured into a muddy lake with fish that attack!

Just Gerdy

G ERDY WAS AN AFRICAN GREY goose, that I had purchased at the local Flee market. Frequently, at night I would hear people partying not far from my house. They played loud music and clearly judging by their music, they were not of the same culture. I decided to purchase Gerdy and her mate to encourage the unwanted partiers to relocate, and it worked. Gerdy and her mate would wander down the road and across the street to the pond then back to my house for some cat food then back to the pond again. This was their daily routine for nearly a month. Then one day Gerdy returned to the house without her mate. For the next 3 weeks, Gerdy went up and down the road honking for her mate. Knowing that wild geese mate for life, I was concerned she had lost her mate for life—my heart ached for her. I even searched the area with her without luck.

After 3 weeks, of watching the gut wrenching honking of Gerdy crying for her mate I decided to try and find another mate for Gerdy. I located a younger grey goose at a local farm. I released this goose from it's transport cage, Gerdy attacked it and attempted to hold it's head under the water for long periods of time. As a few days passed, Gerdy began to accept this goose and she headed down the road to the pond with the new grey goose following her. In the morning, Gerdy was at the house to eat her am cat food, but her new mate was missing. Never to be seen again. Gerdy didn't take the lost of this gander as hard as her first mate. I rationalized that her first mate was very special goose. So I searched the countryside to find a third goose for Gerdy. This time I didn't find another goose but instead I brought home a large white duck named Donald. Gerdy was a bit kinder to Donald and even allowed him to go along for our nightly walks. I use to walk my 2 dogs and my white wolf every evening, around this secluded neighborhood. Gerdy had decided she would come along. Oddly, the dogs all allowed her to walk with us. My only neighbor would occasionally drive by and refer to my evening walk as "Patti's Parade". Red Dawg would lead the way, Maggie (the wolf) would walk on the leash, with Heidi dog and Gerdy next to each other and Donald duck in the rear. This walk was almost a mile and Gerdy always kept up with the pack. After a few months, Donald went missing. I began to wander if I had a "killer goose"—since all her mates kept disappearing. It was at this point I stopped finding mates for Gerdy. I decided it would just have to be Gerdy alone.

The time came that I needed to move closer to my job, so I relocated to Astor Florida. Yes Gerdy moved with me and the dogs. At this location, it was a dirt road we had to walk and it was in a crowded neighborhood. All my neighbors would watch my dogs, Gerdy and myself walk the neighborhood. One time a neighbor yelled to me asking if that was "Aflac" following me.

If I attempted to leave the yard, when Gerdy wasn't looking she would quickly notice I was gone and fly up behind me. In fact she acquired this bad habit of flying behind my Volkswagon car when I was leaving for work. I would drive down the road and look in the rearview mirror only to see Gerdy flying directly behind the car. I would have to stop, turn around and park in the driveway and tell Gerdy to stay and she would. It was uncanny the way she understood the spoken word.

One time when walking in the neighborhood, a loose hunting dog came running towards my walking pack of dogs and goose.

Gerdy took to flight and began circling in the air slightly above us. The neighbor came and grabbing the loose dog. At that point I said playfully "Gerdy get down". And she did. I was stunned! The neighbor said "that's a well trained bird". I had never trained this goose. I replied, "Oh that's just Gerdy".

One time, while attending the Boat Christmas Parade in Astor located on St. John's River, two women approached me and one pointed it's you, she then looked at her friend and introduced me as "The woman who walks with her goose".

At times my neighbors would take pictures of Gerdy walking by their house and text to their families out of state. Everyone seemed to enjoy watching Gerdy just be Gerdy.

After a few months of living there, I purchased a motorcycle and parked it outside my window. Gerdy quickly decided she was to guard that motorcycle and she would sleep by it and circle it, occasionally leaving to eat and take a dip in the plastic swimming pool. Then back to the motorcycle. This caused some problem for the neighbor lady, because every time she would walk outside her house Gerdy would fly at her and attempt to bite her pant leg. She had to use her large garbage barrels to dodge behind, as she walked to her car. It was like the rodeo clowns use their barrels to avoid the bucking bulls. I would hear the yelling (HELP) from outside my house and I would open the window and yell "Gerdy stop"! Gerdy would stop chasing the neighbor then return to guard my motorcycle. Luckily, my neighbor had a good sense of humor, and liked Gerdy and never reported to authorities about her constant goose attacks.

Once again the time came to move (due to employment reasons) and I returned back to my old rental house in Ocklawaha. Life went on with evening walks to include 3 dogs, Gerdy and occasional a stray cat.

It was a hot July morning when I went outside to feed Gerdy only to discover she was gone! I walked back and forth in my neighborhood daily, yelling out her name "Gerdy". This pacing up and down the road, went on for months, I was constantly yelling for Gerdy. My heart ached for this unique pet to return. She never returned! One day as I walked the road yelling for Gerdy I thought of the irony of how Gerdy had paced up and down this same road yonking for beloved mate.

SNAKE EYES

THE SIGN READ "No vehicles beyond this Point, Bridge Out". We had driven over 50 miles to the Cocoa Wildlife Management Area to go fishing.

My boyfriend, his good buddy Dano and I stood looking at one another. I noticed both of them displayed that squinted eye look. You know that look that comes with a mighty hangover and your head aches too much too open your eyes all the way. So you walk around with that "snake eye look" all day until your hangover subsides. We had all had a large time at a Biker Party the night before even through our original plans were to just go fishing on Sunday. Then we learned about the Saturday night party and we decided to attend just for a little while, which lead to a long while, and in to the wee hours of the morning. Now we looked dazed and amazed at each other and the thought of having to hike a mile to the river in the Florida heat. No one wanted to admit that they were too tired and hung over for a mile hike and have to endure the teasing all the way back home. So we agreed to hike to the river. There was little talk as we hiked to the river, just the occasional point to the wild cows that ran the wilderness area. And of course the side stepping to avoid stepping into the large newly deposited cow patties.

It took about an hour to make it to the river and the bridge. We noticed that we could still utilize the bridge if we walked only on the healthily blanks. We had to avoid any with cracks or around any missing board areas. At last we had made it. Dano fished on what was left of the bridge, I fished across the bridge on the bank and my boyfriend fished on the other bank.

It was 30 minutes into this fishing trip that I had turned around to glance at the others to see if they were having any luck. Thank God for my curious mind that day, as I turned around I saw it. It was a snake and it was only a moment from being behind my ankles. This wasn't any OLE snake, no this was a dragon of snakes, this was a 6-foot long diamond back rattlesnake. This dragon looking reptile actually rendered me speechless for a few seconds. I had never seen that large of a snake ever (not in captivity or in the wild)! As I attempted to speak to warn the others, words would not flow from my mouth, instead I made whooping sounds as I skip bounced around the snake in an attempted to confuse the snake and escaped from my cornered spot. I continued with this skip dance past the snake towards my boyfriend, when Dano suddenly was able to interrupt whooping sounds and yell for my boyfriend that there was a snake. I had just made it to my boyfriend just as he ran past me. Whoops I had misjudged him as a safety net and quickly leaped into an old abandoned rowboat.

At this point in time, the snake turned and crawled on to the bridge, towards Dano and coiled with his rattles singing. Dano grapped the only weapon he had, the fish net and threw it on top of the snake. Needless to say, that pissed the snake off even more. My boyfriend yelled for me to throw him the paddle from the rowboat I was still hiding in. I tossed him the paddle, he hit the now coiled rattlesnake and the paddle broke. As for the snake, he now was in possession of the fishing net, the broken paddle, was in control of the bridge. We were all stuck on "the other side of the bridge". This 6-foot rattlesnake was winning! We were trapped, on the wrong side of the bridge! That was more that my boyfriend could bear, he raced over to a over sized corner fenced post and proceeded to pull it out of the ground with the brute strength of a bear hug. He then ran over to the still coiled snake and struck it. Dano made it past the snake to the tackle box, got the filet knife and swiftly cut its head off.

Soon we returned back to fishing, side by side on the bridge, I happened to notice all 3 of us were holding our poles with both hands and in order to control the lingering adrenaline shakes.

The hike back to the truck happened at a much slower pace, as we carefully watched where we placed each foot. I happened to notice on the hike back that out eyes were suddenly wide open as we scanned each cow patty for snake eyes!

THE SURPRISE BUGGY

I T WAS A CHRISTMAS SURPRISE, a pony buggy, given to me by my boyfriend for Christmas! Although I didn't own a pony, I did have a donkey. The pony buggy was awesome gift, it fit my donkey (Poncho) perfectly. So on Christmas Day I hooked Poncho to the buggy and began taking him up and down the sand road in front of my farm home.

After a few trial runs up and down the road, Poncho appeared to be well trained. It was time to take my sister for a ride. So Judy climbed in the buggy and up and down the road we went with smiles on our faces-it was fun. Next was my Dad's turn, then my brother-in-law turn, then my Mom's turn. My Mom required a little bit of encouragement, however after she spoke about her horse Toby her and her brothers had as children she soon lost her fears and climbed into the buggy.

The ride was going along well until a guy on a dirt bike, came up behind us and stopped his engine. He stopped right behind Poncho's harness blinders. He chatted about his new dirt bike and we chatted about the new Christmas buggy.

We wished each other a Happy Holiday and he started his bike. That motor started and Poncho began to trot down the road and my Mom stated "OH this is faster and kinda fun". Then Poncho broke into a gallup, I pulled back on the reins yelling "Whoa" and

Poncho began to pick up speed, So I stood up and pulled hard on the reins, yelling at him to stop. As I pulled back, the right rein broke free causing me to loose my balance and fell into the front of the buggy. I am now tumbling about in the floor board of the buggy, as Poncho began darting back and forth across the road, my mother snatches the other rein out of my hand, and begins yelling "Whoa Poncho" this turns the buggy and Poncho into the forest, pass several trees, as I tumble about struggling to get my foot hold and get back in my seat. Suddenly, Poncho runs between two close trees and the buggy gets stuck! The ride is over! We both got out of the buggy and walked the donkey and the buggy back home. Luckily no one was hurt, that includes Poncho. As for the buggy it was safe but the harness needed repair.

A few weeks later the harness was repaired and it was time for a trial run. I jumped in the buggy, yelling for Mom to get in and try it again. I guess no one was surprised when Mom turned down the buggy ride and walked behind it.

BJ AND THE COWBOY

BJ (SHORT FOR BEAR JUNIOR) was a 85 pound red nose Pit Bull mixed with Bull Mastiff. When this dog entered the room, everyone looked.

His head was huge and most people would spontaneously say out loud "That's a big head!" But it wasn't just BJ's big head that caught everybody's attention; he had a personality that radiated about him. He walked with a fearless stride as if he owned the world yet he still processed a sense of humor that revolved around him. He didn't care for closed doors, and frequently would open the closed bathroom door just to let you know he can do it. Then when he realized he knew the person sitting on the toilet, he demanded a petting moment with the attitude of I found you, you can't resist petting me right? In addition, BJ had a habit when he had misbehaved and he knew he was in trouble, he would hide his head under the couch cushion.

This dog was convinced that if he couldn't see me, I couldn't see him, even through the rest of his 85 pounds of body, was in front of the couch, only his head was missing. He always acted shocked when I lifted the cushion to find his head he had thought that he had so cleverly hidden.

BJ had one great fear, it was to thunder storms. He didn't want to be alone when the lightening flashed and the thunder roared he would shake uncontrollably at bad storms. Back in the mid 1990's, a wicked storm moved south to Florida from the northeast-many called it "The Storm of the Century". This storm bought a lot of devastation as it came south across the states. It hit our home in the middle of the night. The thunder banged loudly and the lightening flashed through the house almost symonateosly with the thunder.

It was around 2:00 am, when I became fully awake from the storm, prior to that I had drifted in and out of sleep. It was this loud band of thunder that awaked me; I sat up in bed. The electric had gone off. I was blinded by the sudden darkness, the only vision I had was during the lightening strikes. Suddenly, I saw him. Something was leaning over the footboard of this old bed. I awaken my boyfriend, he glance in the light of the lightening, as I whispered "Somebody's in here". He saw him too, he appeared to be wearing a cowboy hat, and leaning over the bed. My boyfriend whispered back, "It's a Cowboy, just lay still". Then came another lightening strike, the Cowboy was still in a frozen stance leaning over the bed. My hands began to sweat, as I whispered "What should we do?' Before my boyfriend could answer, another lightening strike revealed a long holster draped across the Cowboy's right shoulder. At the same time we both whispered: "His got a gun!" Our bodies froze in silence, both of us very frighten as we attempted to formulate a plan to overcome this storm prowling Cowboy with a gun. Then 3 more lightening strikes hit flashing brightness into the room, BJ was scared too, whimpering for my touch to calm him. It was after the 3rd lightening flashed that I yelled out loud with laughter in my voice, I said "Look it's not a Cowboy, it's my coat rack that I keep my Cowboy hats on, and that's antique gun holster". BJ must have become frightened and in the process of coming in the bedroom, he knocked the coat rack onto the bedboard. We laughed! Both greatly relieved that it wasn't a storm prowler dressed like a Cowboy. As for BJ, he seemed to calm down, when he heard our laughter, just content that his humans would protect him this wicked storm. Little did he know, we had been scared shitless of our own storm cowboy.

EYES BIGGER THEN HIS STOMACH

"THAT's A BIGGIN" THE WAITRESS stated as she came back through the restaurant door. She had been speaking with a couple of men a few tables over. My boyfriend and I were having breakfast in a local diner in Astor, Florida. Astor, Florida was located on the St. John's River well known for it's large alligator population. We exited the restaurant at the same time as these local men. Sure enough, in the back of their truck was a 12 ½ foot alligator still alive but strapped in. These men were licensed gator trappers and this gator had become a nuisance in a neighborhood full of children.

As I cautiously, stepped closer to their truck and 16-foot Jon boat, I noticed that this low-sided metal boat was riddled with holes all along the top edges of the boat. At that moment I realized what I was looking at, teeth marks—multiple gator bites everywhere. WOW! The men shared a few stories how the marks all got there. I stood in astonishment! Just when you think your work environment sucks, you run across someone, who has a much worse work environment than yours.

I questioned the men about the gator skull and they allowed me to purchase it for $20.00 with a legal certificate. I agreed to meet the man at this restaurant next Saturday. When Saturday arrived, one

27

of the men did meet us at the diner and tossed the gator head in the back of the truck. I must admit I was a bit startled at what I saw. I was expecting a white totally clean keepsake memory of a Florida gator. What I got was a sawed off head of a gator, all skin still intact to include the eyeballs. As we drove away, my boyfriend offered to toss it out in the woods somewhere stating I know you didn't expect this. He was right, I expected a skull to hang near an old cow skull I had on the porch. However, I protested the head tossing and stated I had taxidermy books at home that could help. My boyfriend made it very clear that his participation ended if we didn't toss the head.

When we returned home, I discovered that I would have to peel the skin away from the bone skull with a knife, than place it high off the ground for the black beetles to eat the rest of the meat. The old way of allowing ants to process this skull would break down the bone. The other way I had heard of, to boil the skull, was also not recommended since this method would also break the bone apart. I called our neighbor Steve, since he was a local hunter and requested his help. He arrived at our house a few minutes later. He eyeballed the gator head and agreed to help to peel the hide off the gator head with me. My boyfriend informed us both that his stomach couldn't handle this procedure and decided he would remain in the house. So we drank a few beers and began to scrap the hide away. The hide resembled the constancy of a pineapple, and was difficult to cut. We managed and told jokes and we were making progress, occasionally my boyfriend would peek outside at us wondering if we had abandoned this idea yet then make a statement "You all ain't right, your just not right" then gag and run back in doors. That kept us laughing and we continued to peel the hide away. My side was getting done quicker, so it was time to remove the eyeball. Being a nurse, I have been exposed to many gross body wounds and situations so I seldom think twice about what might be gross to others. At that moment, I cut the eyeball out, holding this giggly blob in my hand and stretched it out to

Steve, and said, "look something was wrong with his eye, look at the darkness". As Steve looked at this hand full of gator eye, he turned a funny white color and turned his head and began to vomit. I felt really bad and began to apologize. When Steve stopped vomiting he turned towards me and confessed "Patti, I really can't stomach this either, I normally take killed deer meat to the butcher. So I finished the gator skull myself and locked it on top of the boat shed so the black beetles to complete the cleaning. I had to lock it in place so that larger critters wouldn't run off with it. Months later it became a trophy gator head. Now when I look at this gator head I always think back to the memory of how this eyeball was too big for Steve's stomach!

HE JUST KNEW

I HAD TAKEN A JOB IN Gallup NM for 13 weeks. I would stay in a Motel from Monday thru Friday then travel back to my rental home in Mancos, CO for the weekend. So every Sunday, my dogs (both rescued years ago, from Florida dog pound) Maggie and Red Dawg would travel to the motel for our weekly stay.

Every morning, Red Dawg and I would drive a few blocks to the local restaurant for breakfast then back to the motel to drop him off and of to work I would go. I might add this was my morning ritual back in Florida too. Off to the Dam Diner, Red Dawg riding shotgun in my little black Volkswagon bug, in would wait until breakfast was over and back to the house for the day. I suffered critizism from both male and female friends due to the large volume of Red Dawg hair that remained in my car after Red Dawg exited. You see Red Dawg was a Chow/ Rottweiler mix. He had that long red Chow hair coat and that large head of a Rottweiler. He honestly looked like Cujo from Stephen King's rabid dog movie.

The truth be known his intimating look did not match his Lassie disposition.

One particular October morning, his Lassie personality actually saved my life. No I hadn't fallen in a well and neither did Timmy (you know the boy from the TV series "Lassie" who would fall in the well and Lassie would rescue him).

What happen that morning was the normal routine, 6 am alarm but this time I shut it off and rolled over. I laid in bed total exhausted just not wanting to get up, I rationalize that I was getting too old to work this hard. I had been working Hospice care on a Navajo reservation and it was slightly exhausting. So I continued to lay in bed when suddenly Red Dawg began pushing on me, and whining, then nodging me more. When that didn't work he stuck his head under the covers and began pushing me with his wet nose up and down the side of my body. I admit, I yelled at him 3 different times to stop and go lay down and he ignored me, which was highly unusual for him, he is a very obedient dog.

Since he wouldn't let me sleep, I forced myself to get up and went to the bathroom. Red Dawg continue to bump my knees while I sat on the toilet. I rationalized that he must be hungry. I staggered to his dish and fed him and Maggie. However, Red Dawg didn't eat his food, instead he continued to follow me. At that time I stumbled into the bathroom and checked my blood sugar (yes I am a Diabetic and on oral medications for this disease) it read "10" and flashed "low". I couldn't believe my eyes then concluded my glucometer must be broken because a reading of "40" or below would have placed into a diabetic coma.

I did notice that I was extremely dizzy and exhausted. I followed my normal routine, I got dressed and put the leash on Red Dawg. I notice he was acting kind of strange. You see normally he would have to urinate on the fence twice then get in the vehicle, but today he literally dragged me to the vehicle and got right in. We only had to drive a few blocks to the local restaurant and 4 different times he reached his paw over as if he wanted to shake my hand, so I shook his paw and thought about how he hadn't done the paw shake trick in years. After a large glass of orange juice and my normal breakfast, my thoughts began to clear and dizziness subsided. I return back to the Motel room and checked my glucometer only to discover it had been working fine. Red Dawg had literally saved my life, by not allowing me to slip into a coma, then to my death.

The next night my boyfriend called and I explained what had happened, still in shock of the whole situation. As I attempted to rationalize Red Dawg's behavior, my boyfriend interrupted me and stated "He just Knew, sometimes dogs just know".

That night Red Dawg, got a couple extra scratches on his head per my boyfriends instruction. And I gave my rescuer, a couple of extra doggie treats. And life went on for the both of us.

MAGIC OF THE SEA

I T WAS A BALMY FLORIDA August afternoon; I headed for the Flagler Pier to fish. The guys at the Pier informed me that the fish had stopped biting a few hours ago. A few large Fishing Rods were placed into, cut off PVC pipes attached to the pier with bungy cords. The guys were right, nothing was biting! Anthony (a regular on the pier) and his buddy Aaron (another frequent Flagler fisherman) were both complaining of no fish and soon said their good-byes and left. A guy whose nickname was "Byrd" also wandered off the pier to the local bar for some drinks, leaving his big game rod he had named "Black Beauty" still baited in the water.

Johnny (the local bait storeowner) lingered on the pier a bit longer, along with a few unknown other fisherman. Johnny processed an uncanny knowledge of the sea and the various fish and their habits that lived there. I wondered if in his past life, he had actually lived in the Sea. Johnny always had this smile on his face as if he had more secret knowledge he hadn't shared yet.

I began to complain of the lack of fish biting when I playfully pointed my hand at my rod and said, "poof" as if to send magic to the pole and stated "I'd even take a shark right now". Suddenly, I got a bite; I raced to my pole, to pull in a small black tip shark. I sat back down, and playfully "poofed" the big game rods. Nothing happened. Johnny complained of a headache and announced he was leaving. Just as he packed up his fishing rods and began to stroll a short distance down the pier, Byrd's rod (Black Beauty) began to sing. I ran to it first only to see the fishing line sailing out to sea. Johnny heard it too and ran back to Black Beauty, grabbing the rod out of the PVC pipe attached to the pier. The line continued to sail straight out as Johnny held tight to the rod. His arm muscles shook as he struggled with the rod; he placed his thumb on the fishing line in an attempt to slow the line. His thumb was quickly burned from the fiery of the pull of the fish on the other end. Whatever it was pulling that line was big, real big! A small crowd gathered around to watch this monster fish get landed. Everyone was guessing what kind of fish it might be, a tarpon, a king, or a shark. A Georgia man questioned me, what I thought it might be, and I soon bet him a whole 50 cents that it was a shark not a tarpon.

Johnny fought that fish back and forth from right to left at the end of the pier. Soon Byrd returned to see that it was Black Beauty (his rod) that was the center of attention. He grabbed the gaff and chased Johnny, and his fishing pole back and forth on the pier. Johnny's Texas determination shined through his eyes, he was going to win this fight with the fish. After 40 minutes, the monster on the other end showed himself—it was a 7-foot black tip shark. The shark was now at the pier and the gaff was ready. Suddenly, the line just snapped, sending the 5-½ ounce claw lead weight into the air and dropping on to the pier. The battle was over, the shark had won! He returned to the sea. Bryd returned to the shore for another drink to toast the event that happened on his rod. Johnny wandered off the pier with that same smile just much larger! As for me, I waved goodbye with 2 quarters in my hand thinking "ahhhhhhhh" the Magic of the Sea!

Bet on the Yellow Jackets

As my friend and I descended down the hill in the back of the house we were headed for the picnic table to watch the colorful sunset across Lake Sellers. My picnic table sat near the lake's edge under several twisted oak trees. Giving the area a spooky feel to it. The crystal clear lake seem to accent the glowing colorful sunset, bringing out the reds, yellows and purples. Witnessing these extraordinary sunsets will forever be etched in my memory. Sometimes as the sun was setting, the Florida Bass would jump out of the water splashing their tails on the Lake's surface.

Today as we walked towards the picnic table we spotted a different tail; it was only a few feet in front of us. It was the tail of a pigmy rattlesnake. Surrounding this snake was a large amount of yellow jacket bees. They were repeatedly stinging the rattlesnake. The snake was still alive, yet becoming very weak. Since yellow jackets make their nest in the ground, we speculated that this snake, while crawling through the forest, must have crawled across a yellow jacket's nest and that was all it took to piss this pack of bees off.

We cautiously went to the lake, the bees seemed only interested in the snake so we both made it past without getting stung. We enjoyed our sunset, moaning as the color's intensified. As this day began to reach that twilight hour, we ventured back up the hill, watching carefully for the pigmy rattlesnake, to avoid being bitten. There it was, laying still on the ground-LIFELESS! The yellow jackets had stung this poisonous snake to death. We stared in amazement! This snake had met its venomous match. I wondered about the karma in this situation. I would have bet on the rattlesnake. Who knew?

RETURN OF SILLY BEAR

I WAS TRAVELING EAST ON HIGHWAY 40, traveling from Ocala area though Astor area, to have dinner by the St. John's River. As I drove through the Ocala National Forest, I disassociated into deep thought, regarding my living situation. I was back in Florida from Colorado, the employment offer I had returned to Florida for, had collapsed. I was seriously doubting my decision. I had traveled to the Rocky Mountains 3 separate times to live in the last 3 years. I now wondered where my home really was. Where would I feel comfortable living again? I have friends in Florida, Colorado and in my home State of Michigan. Suddenly, I saw something black in the distance on the left side of the road. As I approached closer I realize I had spotted a bear—a very, very, large black bear! I pulled off the right side of the road to observe this enormous bear, when I began to realize that this wasn't any Florida black bear this was "Silly Bear".

Silly Bear and I met over 10 years ago. He had wandered on to my farm and was chasing my farm animals around. He appeared to have lost his fear of humans at that time and it greatly concerned me. He was wearing a tracking collar back then, indicating he had been a nuisance bear somewhere and given a collar for tracking. What I didn't know at the time was that he had been abandoned by this mother bear, actually raised by a man who had lived a few miles through the forest from my house. This man had fed him corn and dog food since he was a small bear cub. That is why he became such a large bear. I had called Fish and Game and they soon darted him and removed him from the area.

However, in the process of taking him to another forest up in Tallahassee, he had escaped from a pen leaving his electronic collar hanging on the chain link fence. I happened to catch a brief news clip, a few days after Silly Bear had been darted, showing this bear collar hanging on the fence. I knew it had to have been Silly Bear's collar.

I had called him "Big Bear" since I had discovered his tracks weeks before I actually had an encounter with him. Both my fists could fit into just one bear track. He was real big! The first time I had actually seen him I recall running in the house saying out loud "That's a big bear!" What I didn't know at that time was that he actually was a neighbor's pet. It was a month later, while being introduced to people in the local bar that I met Silly Bear's Dad. That is when I learned his name to be Silly Bear, because of his playful habits of tossing a football into the air until deflated by his claws. His Dad apparently keeps extra on hand. This particular day, that I encountered Silly Bear was when his man friend was in Orlando for the weekend. Silly Bear had entered this man's house and dragged his lazy Boy recliner deep in to the forest. This man reported that he tracked the chair tracks for hours and never found it. I truly regretted at that time that I had Silly Bear removed but I hadn't known he had been slightly tamed.

Now 10 years later, there he was—Silly Bear standing across the road from me. He had that same stand, holding his left paw slightly up, sniffing the air, with a hunch to his back. I knew like I knew like I knew, this was Silly Bear! He had returned home. More importantly he wasn't wearing a nuisance collar. Perhaps he had learned a healthy respect for humans. I looked around and realized that I was only a few miles from my old farm. Silly Bear had returned home!

Just then a truck passed, Silly Bear bolted back into the woods. As I ate dinner, I began to contemplate the coincidence of seeing Silly

Bear as I was wondering where my home should be. A few weeks later, I rented a home in Astor. As I began moving to my new house, I pulled in the driveway of my new place, it was near dusk. I heard a peculiar sound; I listened again, identifying the sound as a unique cell phone ring. Then I heard it again, it was the hoot of an owl, and I am convinced I was being welcomed back to the Ocala Forest the place I called home over 10 years ago. I look forward to day that I stumble across an old recliner buried deep in the woods!!!

THE WHISTLE

I CURRENTLY SPEND MY WINTERTIME IN a rustic cottage, located in Salt Springs Florida. My cottage is located on the shores of Lake George (the second largest lake in Florida). This area has an abundance of wildlife to include bald eagles, osprey, foxes, raccoons, bobcats, a variety of snakes and black bear.

There were a total of 3 black bear that lived in this neighborhood area. One in particular was a large black bear, I frequently referred to as Albert (you know, like fat Albert). This bear must have weighed 800 pounds. When walking my dog Maggie one evening, we walked up to the road and only a few feet in front of me was Albert. When Albert saw me, he just sat down. Right there in front of me. There we stood until he finally got up and walked around me down the road.

A few days later early in the morning as I approached my car, I noticed that both passenger side doors were opened. I walked around the car worried that My car had been broke into. As I studied the car for damaged I noticed a paw print on the back door next to the door knob. It was a bear print! Albert had opened my Kia Soul door, looking for food I guess. However, they advertise these cars as being pet friendly but this is too much!!

I drove into town for breakfast only to return to see Albert sitting across the street from my cottage. He was staring at my cottage, sitting with his belly hanging out, as if he was an old man, whittling a stick or whistling as he waited.

That evening my 95 year old neighbor had an encounter with Albert. Albert was pulling on her trailer side door @ 2:30 am. She awakened and pushed the door against the bear knocking him off her porch. Off he ran into the forest.

The next evening when I returned from work the Fish and Game officer was standing with my elderly neighbor and another lady from the neighborhood discussing how the bear had pulled my neighbors door off. As we spoke the officer motioned for us to be quiet as he spotted the smaller bear crossing the street only a few feet away from us. We reassured the officer that the 3 bears that roamed this neighborhood were not scared of our voices. As the bear walked back and forth across the street in front of us he soon learned we were right. As we discussed which bear performed the home invasion, I believed it was Albert (the sit down bear), the other neighbor believed it was the little bear. Just then a 4 wheel drive pick—up pulled up and introduced himself as the neighbor that lived behind us behind the fence. He reported that Albert had taken a bag of Doritos from him the other night. He stated "I was sitting in my carport having a beer and eating from a large bag of Doritos when that large black bear came into my carport and sat down not far from me. That's when I realize I had the only food source, so I threw him one dorito chip, he ate it and I threw the rest of the bag down as he had his attention focused on eating the one chip and I was able to escape into the house". "He is taking food right out of our mouths!" He reports that the bear finished the bag and wander off to another neighbor' house. The officer stated he had something for him and my elderly neighbor. He went to his truck and dug into a bag. My first thought was he is gonna pull out a stun gun or a form of a tazer. I was wrong, I stood stunned as he pasted out 2 large orange whistles. He instructed that the sound of the whistle will scare the bear off.

For the next 2 nights, I lay in bed listening to the both of them blow in that whistle over and over. Clearly, it didn't scare the bear and 2 days later no more whistle. As I left for work early in the am I looked at the pile of bear shit he had once again deposited near my cottage, but this time I looked close—pondering the question was there a orange whistle in that pile????

THE DUCKS

As I danced around the carport of my new home in the Ocala Forest, my boyfriend sat drinking a beer and we both enjoyed the gentle summer night. I had successfully raised baby ducks to adult ducks and today I had released them into the wild to share the lake with me. I was very pleased!

Just then my boyfriend screamed the word "Duck", as I turned one of my ducks had returned to the carport flying in at head height. That is when it hit me! I had never given any thought to the fact that humans would yell out a wild bird's name when something was about to fall on your head.

I had to wonder what situation one would be in when someone yells "Duck, Duck Goose"!!!!!

TAILS TOLD BY OTHERS

WHOSE GOT THE BUTTON

FLORIDA PEOPLE COMMONLY PARTY IN their yards; all you need is a grill, cooler full of beer and a campfire. The campfire smoke aids in controlling the biting mosquitoes and the fire adds an atmosphere for the telling of tales. One particular tale has always stuck in the archives of my memory, unfortunately the name of the guy who told the story I have forgotten. The following is his story:

He told of going to Texas with his wife, to attend a family members wedding. He said he got dressed in his suit and was mighty proud of being dressed before his wife, for once. Apparently, he had a habit of being late and the last one dressed. So he went outside to wait on the patio of his family's farm. He was relaxing drinking a beer, when a large EMU walked up to him. The EMU appeared to be very interested in his appearance and lowered his head as if to stare directly into his eyes. He stared and smiled back at the EMU, having a sensation of man and beast bonding. Feeling very moved by this bonding moment he let his guard down allowing this large bird to come closer. Then suddenly in a moment's notice this bird lowered his head and was able to remove every button off his dress shirt, with great precision. He quickly stood up looked down at his now wide open buttonless dress shirt when his wife walked out of the house and said "I'm ready"!

THE RIVER RIDE

THIS STORY WAS ALSO TOLD at Florida yard party. While boating in a pontoon boat down the St. John's River. (This river is known for it's brackest waters and it's abundant fish, gator, snake, and manatee population). One particular day, several friends were drinking and having a party time in the Florida sun, when they spotted a manatee swimming along side their pontoon boat and diving in and out of the water like a dolphin frequently does. All stood in amazement watching this entertaining sight when suddenly one of the redneck southern boys on the boat had a bonding moment with this large beast and proceeded to dive into the water and grabbed hold of this manatee's back. At that moment, he became acutely aware that the Manatee's skin had a friction type rub to it and between the skin and the movement of this swimming beast it ripped his "drawers" right off him. From that day forward, all those observing this event, have a new image of that magical being "The Mermaid", it suddenly change to an overweight naked southern man riding on the back of a manatee grabbing at the sky in an attempt to catch his cap that just blew off his head.

From that moment on, Dan was known as "Danatee!

TURBO

THIS STORY WAS AIRED ON the Florida local NBC am news back in December 2010. It touched my soul, I hope it touches yours.

It seems Turbo was a name of a dog that had fallen into the salty deep canal in the front of his masters house. Turbo could not get out of the steep boarded banks of the canal. Turbo had been missing for over 24 hours when a neighbor noticed in the canal, a pod of dolphins taking turns lifting a black animal above the waters. The neighbor went out to investigate only to discover it was his neighbors dog— "Turbo". The neighbor assisted with the rescue of Turbo and he was returned to his master save and sound. The dolphins playfully swam away.

WOW animals saving animals—now that's awesome. I made a point to watch the evening news hoping to catch a glimpse of this very special dog. The news did show Turbo, a black Doberman mix with one ear up and one ear drooping down. He had a playful look to him, which brought a smile to my face, I had expected some magical being, instead he was just an overexcited young Doberman. Who now is afraid of water! GO DOLPHINS!!!!!!!

TAILS OF THE SPIRIT

A FOREST CAROL

"THIS IS WHERE WE RELOCATE PROBLEM BEARS" the Fish and Game officer stated. Isn't that odd, I thought to myself, the realtor never mentioned that outstanding piece of information when he was showing me this property. "I guess that explains the electronic collar the black bear was wearing.

The incident occurred last night; it was a warm Florida night. We were sitting relaxing under the carport, when we heard sudden movement in the pasture. We quickly went to the pasture to observe a black bear being chased across the pasture by Poncho my pet donkey (better known as a Palestine burro). I stared in utter amazement, as my donkey, bowed his head kicked his rear heels and chased the bear a few feet across the barnyard area, then up a tree. I knew that Florida farmers would frequently used jack donkeys to protect their herds of cattle from coyotes, but from bears—WOW! Then it happened, the bear jumped out of the tree, and began chasing Poncho across the pasture. Poncho's posture changed to an equine full of fear, and his chosen path, you ask? Poncho began running to his place of safety, directly towards me! As my brain processed the fact that a scared donkey and a wild Florida black bear was running directly act me, I froze in fear, which evidently scared the bear, and he made a sudden curve to the left then off to the forest he ran. Poncho's anxiety was calmed after a few carrots and a quick brushing. The night returned to calm warm August night.

Fish and Game were notified the next day. They came to investigate and to inform me that my new farm located in the Ocala National Forest was located directly in the middle of "problem bear territory".

Now that little piece of information may have scared others, but as for me—I planned to adapt and conquer. Poncho was fun to ride, even if my feet were only a short distance from the ground. You see, Poncho had bonded with me, and as all donkey (and mule) owners know, they become pets and some will even protect you on the trails, from harm. When horses spook, they will often run you and them into thickets, brush, holes and other dangerous areas. A pet donkey won't do that.

A week later, Poncho and I were off on our first ride in the forest together. I could feel Poncho shake as we walked and I knew he must be fearful of a possibility of another bear encounter, after all the last one had chased him. So I decided to sing, that way the bears would hear us coming and hopefully avoid us. So I screamed (since I do not pocess a talent for singing) out all the words to the Christmas carols, that I had learned as a child. Poncho clamed down and his gait smoothed out. All was well. Until I stopped singing. Poncho would stop, turn his head all the way back to my boots and tugged on my jeans. When I started singing, he would continue to take me for a ride. It stunned me that he knew that the singing would keep the bears away. Or I wonder, was it much deeper then that? Being a Palestine burro, legend states that the black marking across their shoulders and down their back was a mark given to them by Jesus since this was the breed he rode. I just wonder if he was having some "cellular memory" of those ancient days, and he felt calmed by hearing the words to "Away in the Manager"?

THE EASTER DANCE

I T WAS EASTER SUNDAY, I found myself fishing at the Flagler Pier. What a delight! The Blues were biting, although most were smaller than 12 inches (therefore had to be tossed back) they put up enough fight for a good thrill.

I soon noticed that a pod of dolphins had approached the pier. I watched in amazement as the dolphins dove in and out of the waves. Such graceful playfulness they exhibited! Then suddenly one in particular caught my eye. This dolphin was randomly tossing fish into the air. At first I thought she was teasing all of us. Since the fish she was catching were much larger then anything being caught on the pier this day. Then I saw this dolphin's baby. This mother dolphin was teaching her baby to fish. She would toss the fish into the air then it would fall back to the water stunted from the water's slap. At which time the baby would grab it and eat it. This ritual continued most of the day. At times she would lay only 8 to 10 feet from the pier and just float and stare. Was she watching us fish, did she wonder if we were teaching our young to fish and eat. The truth is some families were teaching or attempting to teach their young sons to focus and fish. It appeared she was more successful at it then the humans were.

Even a large sea turtle swam in to get a better look at the humans on the pier. This day was a true nature show for all. As I was enchanted by the Sea I began to explore how Easter represented the raise of Jesus and the verlasting spirit life. To the pagans this was the holiday of fertility, birth-spring—the new beginning. That's where the bunnies and the chickens come in. Right Now—here in front of me was a dolphin with her baby teaching how to fish for food. The cycle of life was so ever present this day. No Easter basket needed this day—just bait.

TAIL PIPES

THERE ARE TIMES WHEN I would leave the world of gators, snakes and bears and adventure out in to the world to attend biker events from Daytona to Sturgis or just go motorcycle riding with friends. Spending time with true bikers has an animalistic quality all of it own. With encouragement from my biker buddies I have included this section to the book.

The following stories are all true stories dedicated to those I ride with or haven't rode with yet. You all have touched my heart in some way or another. You know who you are and to you—I wish

HAPPY TRAILS!

GOT VODKA

WE (A GROUP OF FRIENDS from Lake and Sumter Counties) called it the campgrounds; it was 5 acres of horse pasture located in Samsula Florida. This campgrounds is where we all gathered twice a year; for Bike week in March and Biketoberfest in October. The main attraction at the campgrounds was the fire pit located near the front of the property. In the evening we would all gather around the fire telling jokes and life stories that had occurred since our last gathering. Laughter was had by all.

It was Bike Week 2010, when I arrived back to the campgrounds from the local bar, when I noticed by the fire, a blonde guy sound asleep with an almost empty half gallon of vodka by his chair. My attempt to arouse him failed, I questioned who he was. Ike informed me that he came with a group of people from Sorrento Florida, and when he passed, they went down to the bar leaving him behind. As some of you may already know, being the first to pass out in a group of partying bikers could have humorous results. And it did! With encouragement from the partying campfire crowd, I placed a open tampon between his fingers, as if he was holding a cigarette, then Rachael put lip stick on it. As we were contemplating other tricks to do to this man, he woke up. He looked around the campfire, we quickly told him he was in South Dakota and that his friends had left. His response was "At least I'm not in Georgia" that brought a few chuckles to all our faces. He then reached into his pocket to get his lighter, placing the tampon with the lipstick end in his mouth, and holding it there while the string dangled from his mouth. Everyone roared in laughter, he looked around thinking someone had told a funny joke and he missed it. As he began to light the object in his mouth he saw the string hanging, never seemed to recognize that it was a tampon, instead he acted as if it was a faulty cigarette he then threw it into the fire. The comment was made, "maybe this has happened to him before." Conversation with this man was limited. He questioned where his friends were and how did he get to South Dakota. Then his phone rang, it was from Ike just sitting across the campfire, but this man's vodka toasted mind could not register the joke being played on him. Ike handed the phone to me, I flirted with him telling him I was coming to see him. It didn't seem to matter he had no clue who I was, I then handed the phone to Rachael, she talked some sex talk to him and he fell for it. Requesting she gets to him as soon as possible, she asked if she could bring a girlfriend or two. He agreed and stated (on speaker phone) that he only had one condom but it could be reused. Laughter roared about the campfire as we listened to his response. Once again he didn't realize that we were laughing at him, as many of us gathered around the phone across the fire from him. As time went on he begin calling the number back, I would answer and told him there were actually three of us. He gave directions again of course missing streets. But he seemed positive he hadn't left Florida. He called back a third time, I asked him his name. He told me and I informed him I thought he was Johnny. He said he didn't know a Johnny, what was his last name? I told him it was Black—"Johnny Black" (a fictitious name). I informed him we were calling for Johnny, not for him. He was so excited about three women, that he informed me that we could call him Johnny he that would work.

As time went on, he sat staring at the driveway awaiting the three women to arrive. Occasionally he would call the number back and we informed him we were on the way. It grew late and I decided to head home, as I left Ike yells out to me "Tell Johnny I said Hello". I chuckled and left. This poor guy never did catch on to the fact that a joke was being played on him and I was told (the next day) that he sat near the fire, with his empty Vodka bottle under his chair, and his one condom awaiting for the 3 unknown women to show up. Gotta wonder about the powers of Vodka?????

WHOSE GOT THE PANTIES

BIKE WEEK FALLS DURING THE first full week of March in Daytona Beach, Florida. That is when the motorcycle races are held. As the years went by the admission prices skyrocketed so attending the races became an event of the past, but the partying continued. As for my group of riding friends we would all gather at a horse pasture just outside of Daytona Beach, we all referred to this location as the "campgrounds". It was a horse and cow pasture during the other 50 weeks of the year. However, the guys did all gather together one year and with donations and guidance of my buddy Ike and they made a portable (out of wood) shower and bathroom. They loaded it up on the back of a bike trailer and hauled to the campgrounds. The motivation to build must have been from the 14 day smell of the men and woman that would manage to camp in this rustic setting. So now the campground was official—we had a bathroom, yhea!

At night we would all come in from our riding adventures and warm our bones and our souls near the fire. (Yes it can get down in the 30's in March in Fl). We would tell stories about riding adventures and of course about our adventures or misadventures to Sturgis Motorcycle Rally in SD (that is held the first full week in Aug. Ike who was one of the older bikers (sorry Ike) along with Lucas (another old school biker) would always be found at the campgrounds. Both would gather funny jokes thru the year for the telling at the campfire. Lucas would also present information from the Discovery channel that clearly he had not missed an episode in a long time. Being discovery channel deprived, I would always leave Bike Week with a lot of information I could never use (like the existence of concrete boats etc.).

One year, Ike was in the mood for playing jokes on people. It was all laughs until in targeted me for a couple of days. So I decided to play back! I might add it was against my boyfriend's wishes (he and Ike were and still are best of friends). I found a pair of underpanties, fancy ones and placed them under Ike's pillow in his van. You see, Mary his current girlfriend at the time, was due to arrive for the Bike Week festival today. Mary was my good buddy, so I decided to call her and let her in on the joke, informing her of all the practical jokes Ike had played on me. She was all for it and agreed to play along.

Meanwhile, at the campfire Ike holding a cute yard ornament, that he had purchased for a surprise gift for Mary, bragged about how kind Mary will be to him for this special gift. I might add, he meant it in a sexual nature. Everyone at the campfire knew about the panties under Ike's pillow, except for Ike at that time. There must have been at least 30 of us laughing at what was about to unfold, that is except for my boyfriend (he was a little worried). I might add, Ike was a big healthy biker guy, a little on the pushy side @ times and very few people ever played back. I might add this underwear joke, was actually a joke Ike had told at the campfire, that he had played on one of his buddies years ago and it ended up in a divorce. Ike said he didn't mean for that to happen.

A few hours went by, and finally Mary arrived in her van. We all sat waiting for Mary to find the panties. After about 45 minutes she found the panties. And the games began. Unknowingly to me, Mary took the game one step farther. She found the panties, acted pissed, and Ike hollered in a loud intimating voice that he was going to "kill Patti". Mary then got in her van and drove off (that wasn't the plan).

I stood stunned and amazed, most people vacated the campgrounds and my boyfriend went to Ike and attempted to explain that it was a joke. Ike then changed his threat to "if Mary isn't back in 5 minutes I'm going to kill Patti". As you might guess, 5 minutes pasted and no Mary. So Ike changed his threat to I'm giving Mary 10 more minutes to return or I'm going to kill Patti". Ike's loud yell echoed thru the horse pasture. Still no Mary! Then came a third threat extending the time limit. Still no Mary! Meanwhile my boyfriend began feeding Ike rum to attempt to settle him down, all the time wondering if he was going to get his ass beat in an attempt to stop Ike from killing me. As for me, I sat with my friend's from Michigan (Paul and Vicky) at the campfire, giggling about how Ike couldn't take a joke.

Finally, a strange motorcycle came riding up the ½ mile dirt road that lead to our campgrounds. He yelled as he sat on his bike "Any of you know a female in a van?" "Cuz she's stuck in a ditch at the beginning of the driveway". We all jumped on our bikes and road down to Mary's van. Mary was not hurt, instead she sat drinking her rum, laughing hysterically. She stated "I didn't mean for this to happen!" I might add neither did I.

The next morning, we gathered at the campfire, Ike and I were forced to make a handshake truce—Never to play jokes on each other again. They said it stressed out my boyfriend too much! I guess it just got his panties in a wad!!!

BUTT DARTS

IT WAS NEWELL, SOUTH DAKOTA, and my boyfriend and I had been riding our scooters for hours. It was over due time for a break. So we decided to stop at a hidden away local bar. There were only a few people in the bar but all were friendly. After drinking a beer all was boring, so in an attempt to break the boredom, I asked the guy next to me "Do you have any special talents? He thought for a moment, then began rolling the bar towel into a shape of something. Then he asked, "what's this look like"? We all yelled at the same time, a penis! So ended his talent. Then the guy next to him said does a special tattoo count? "Sure" I replied. At which point he lowered his pants slightly, to expose the word "your name" tattooed on his left buttocks. That bought a lot of laughter and even more when new people entered the bar. I quickly greeted them and ask the young couple their names. They offered their names and I said I'll bet you 50 cents that the guy over there has your name tattooed on his butt. "Not the way I spell it the guy said". He even foolishly upped the bet another 50 cents. So I agreed, smiling the whole time, I might add. As the tattooed buttocks were exposed, the guy broke out into a roaring laughter and paid me $1.00. He agreed that was the way he spelled "your name". I won several dollars off of this new game I had created, as new people entered the bar, the same routine of questions occurred and a few more times people would say "not the way I spell it" and loose with a smile on their face.

As the game slowed down, people started to ask me if I had any special talents? That is when my boyfriend spoke up and said "She's good at quarters". With in a short period of time, I was demonstrating what this game was all about. I would take a quarter, and place it in the crack of my butt (with my pants on) and proceed to drop it into a glass located on the floor behind me. At the precise moment, that I was demonstrating this game, the door swung open and a female entered and yelled out "Butt Darts". "I'm the champion back in Wisconsin". So the challenge was on! The bar was cheering us both on as we began to compete for the "Queen of Butt Darts". We began with a quarter and a regular bar glass, we tied. Then we moved on to a shot glass and a quarter. She went first, perfect shot. This female was good at this now newly named sport. My turn, I heard the quarter ding the shot glass another tie! The bar cheered and laughed all at the same time!

Then my boyfriend broke out the dime. She went first, dropping the dime directly without any hesitation, into the shot glass. It was my turn, I aimed and dropped the dime, I heard it hit the side of the shot glass, making a dinging sound then suddenly pounce out of the shot glass on to the floor. Too much force I guess, Who knew. She had won! She returned to somewhere, Wisconsin as the "Queen of Butt Darts". As for me, I returned to Florida, with tales about what fun you can have with your own tail!!!

THE DOLLAR

I T WAS ACTUALLY MY BUDDY—IKE's idea. We were at The Cabbage Patch in rural Volusia County, it was Bike week! He provided me a black heavy thread and a crubbled up dollar. He instructed me to attach the dollar to the thread and throw on the dirt path leading to bar. Amazingly many people would chase that dollar, as I pulled slowly towards me. I guess they thought the wind was blowing it. Loud laughter was had by all. Many of those, that had fallen for the dollar chase. Would hang around too watch other people chase the dollar. Soon a crowd would gather and many loud laughs. Occasionally I would pair up with another female and have her stand in the crowd and point to the dirty cruppled dollar after they pass by and say "Hey, I think you lost a dollar". They would turn around and chase it up to the picnic table where I was sitting.

For years, during Bike week I would play this game and many bikers gather to watch the "dollar chase". One day a very good looking female approach the crowd, she was wearing tiny underwear and leather chaps over them. She walked in the opposite direction of the dollar, but the guys around wanted to see her chase the dollar. So the couple that was standing near me decided to help. The blonde female took the dollar and dropped just behind the feet of the female dressed in undies and leather chaps. Then the blonde taps the female on the shoulder to inform her she had dropped a dollar. Her reply was "Could you grab it for me"? So the blonde picked it up to hand to the barely dressed female. I quickly pulled the string, as her ole man roared with laughter. She was apart of the joke and apparently forgot!

I was captured on many people's videos as their friends set each other up to the embarrassment of chasing the dollar. Then one night as I sat waiting for a person to pursue the dollar chase, a female in a wheel chair ran over my dollar and the thread spun around her wheel and he began to drag the dollar across the crowd. I quickly took chase of my own dollar, just then I heard a familiar voice in the crowd—it was Mike yelling to me "Let her have the dollar"! Laughter roared as I realized after all these years I was finally chasing my own dollar!!!!

The Rebel

MY VERY FIRST MOTORCYCLE WAS a 250 Honda Rebel. It was white with a red pin stripe running down the tank. I must admit I was reluctant to buy it. I bought it from Mikes Bike Shop in Dona Vista. Mike had encouraged me to purchase it to learn to ride on. I really didn't want to own a Honda; I wanted my first bike to be a Harley. I made jokes about having to wear a full-face helmet so no one would recognize me on this Honda. For the cost of $700 it was a good deal I had to agree with Mike. So I bought it. (My boyfriend reminded me how for years I refused to date him because his first bike was a Triumph. I use to make jokes with him way back then, about wearing a full face helmet too).

We took the bike to my house in the forest with a mile paved road near by and I would race home from work to practice every night riding my bike up and down that mile stretch. It took me weeks before I actually picked up my speed to shift from 1st to the other gears. But the day came when I finally did. I fell in love with that bike!

Then August came around and it was time for our yearly trip out to the Bike Rally at Sturgis, South Dakota. Several of our friends came over to help us pack for our upcoming cross-country trip.

We would save all year long for this particular event; it was the highlight of my life. I was in love with the West (still am) and the excitement that the Sturgis rally had to offer. Since I was a new rider,

I had planned to continue to ride with my boyfriend, but this year he informed me that my Rebel was to be loaded on the trailer and if I wanted to ride I had to ride my own bike or not ride at all. Needless to say, the Rebel was loaded. The first time I rode my bike on the road with traffic was in South Dakota; we rode away from Sturgis to a little sheep town called Newell. We had breakfast and rode back to the camp. I was very proud of my first successful ride, so that night I decided to indulged in a few shots of whiskey. Feeling cocky I stood up in front of my boyfriend, puffed out my upper arm muscle and pointed to my muscle and stated "Any minute a Tattoos going pop right out". My boyfriend replied: "Yea and it's going say HONDA".

THE
CONCLUSION

LEAP OF FAITH

THIS EVENT HAPPENED AS I was putting my finishing touches on this book. I was so amazed by this story, I felt compelled to end this book with it.

It was 6 years ago, that my orange colored cat I called Cysco, just disappeared. My 3 dogs (Heidi, Red Dawg and Barney) my cat Cysco and I rented a little house in a town in Florida, called "Howey in the Hills". This town is located approximately 80 miles south of the Ocala National Forest. It is in the Forest where I usually reside. My pack and I had returned from a travel assignment out in Colorado. Unable to find a rental in the forest, I rented this little house with a fenced yard, in Howey in the Hills. However, I continued to search unsuccessfully for a place in the forest. I quickly realized that my landlord was not a fan of Cysco. He complained that cats were capable of doing a lot of damage to a home. Cysco was a indoor / outdoor cat and appeared to have no desire to destroy anyone's house. He would come home from his outdoor adventures in the evening time and persistently meow at the front door until I opened the door and let him inside. His routine was very predictable, he would enter the house—first to the kitchen for a few bites of dry cat food, then he would locate Barney, my black standard poodle and lay beside him for the night. I often would joke that Cysco was Barney's cat, not mine.

One evening Cysco didn't return home. I stood outside and called him, no response. Barney also paced the floor. I checked the door several times expecting to see Cysco arriving, just a little late. Still no Cysco. I went to bed that night thinking he would be at the door when I awakened. At daybreak I raced straight to the door expecting to see my hungry cat but he wasn't there. Behind me stood Barney, sniffing the air for a trace of his cat. When the scent revealed no cat he just returned to the front room and laid down in his favorite spot.

As days passed and no return of Cysco, I went to the local animal shelter searching for him. I traveled the neighborhood and posted signs. On the days I couldn't go to the animal shelter, I would call. No sign of Cysco. Every night I would call his name as I walked the neighborhood with Barney beside me.

I searched the ditches in case he had been hurt and couldn't make it home.

I began to suspect that my Landlord (who resided 2 acres behind my rental) had done something to my cat. As days became weeks, and weeks became months I began to believe that he had died. Because I knew my Cysco would never leave me or his canine friend Barney.

I found a rental in Ocklawaha and moved, although I continue to return to my neighborhood in Howey searching for my cat. I continued weekly visits to the animal shelter which always revealed no Cysco. My Cysco must be dead. Because I knew he would never leave his pack.

I was offered a great paying job in Denver and I quickly accepted. Sadly, a week before my travel to Colorado my dog Barney died from a seizure. He was buried in Florida. I believed he had joined his favorite cat in the spirit world. However, the day before I left Florida, I checked the shelter one last time. Still no Cysco!

I did go to Colorado to work. For the next 6 years I worked at travel assignments that resulted in trips to Florida then back to Colorado. It was a busy time of my life. This trip back to Florida, I was offered a Home Health job to visit patients in the Ocala Forest to be "the woods nurse". I quickly accepted the position, since I was renting a cottage in the forest.

In November, a few days before Thanksgiving, I was sent to a home north of Ocala. As I approached the patient's porch I saw an extremely thin orange cat lying on the porch. I casually stated to the family that the orange cat strongly resembled my missing cat from years ago. She looked startled has she explained that the orange cat had arrived at her farm just recently. She explained that this cat sat across the street and meowed all day. When the sun began to set, she stated that she feared that a coyote may kill this wailing cat. She went across the street and carried the cat inside her home. This cat immediately jumped from her arms and began rubbing against her black standard poodle. She was shocked at his lack of fear of her large dog and his shocking fragile condition. She told me, that he had to be treated for respiratory infection, all variety of worms, ticks and fleas. She stated that this cat meowed all day and night for 2 days. She told me "this cat has a story to tell". I began to tell her his story and how I painstakingly searched for him. I explained that he was raised with dogs. I explained that his best friend was a black standard poodle named Barney.

It was when I told her his name (Cysco) she looked shocked and I asked her why the odd look? She explained that her 20 year old cat had died 3 months ago and that cat's name was also Cysco. WOW! The most amazing thing was that this cat arrived sick and starving 3 days before I even knew I was going there. What leap of faith it was for him to travel 80 miles to a location I hadn't been to yet.

Cysco is now home with me. He remembers Red Dawg and rubs against him regularly. I explained to him Barney had died. Oddly, Cysco doesn't even look for Barney. Was it the spirit of Barney or the spirit of her Cysco that lead him to me that day??

Cysco stays on the front porch as he heals both emotionally and physically from his 6 year ordeal. He is always happy to see me and still takes "leaps of faith" when I enter the porch he jumps from his current spot, thru the air, into my chest. So far I've been able to catch him every time!

Sadly, Red Dawg became sick and 4 days later on August 16, 2013, my beloved Red Dawg died. Cysco laid touching him as he passed to the spirit world.

I was heartbroken and judging by Cysco's behavior he was suffering from grief too.

A few days later I went to a Spiritualist and she gave me a reading. She explained that some animal's spirit are meant to follow us thru our life's journey and Red Dawg was a spirit that had been with me in other pets. She handed me a piece of paper and instructed me to write down the following message—"You can not keep him from you". She explained that when his soul returns, he will find me.

Wow! What a concept! She instructed me to do nothing, he will find me. So Cysco and I are faithfully awaiting his spirit return!!! It may be a big leap of faith but one thing Cysco's return has taught me—just have faith!!!!

Printed in the United States
By Bookmasters